LONER FORENSICS

LONER FORENSICS
POEMS

Thea Brown

CURBSTONE BOOKS / NORTHWESTERN UNIVERSITY PRESS
EVANSTON, ILLINOIS

Curbstone Books

Northwestern University Press

www.nupress.northwestern.edu

Copyright © 2023 by Northwestern University. Published 2023 by Curbstone Books / Northwestern University Press.

Printed in the United States of America

10   9   8   7   6   5   4   3   2   1

ISBN 9780810146235 (paper)

ISBN 978081014624-2 (ebook)

Library of Congress Cataloging-in-Publication Data

Cold heart, cold heart, cold heart, cold heart.
[Nirvana]

CONTENTS

Head South, Catafalque   3

The Annotator   14

The Forensics Team   15

The Mayor   16

The Palm Reader   18

The Amateurs   20

The Cultural Anthropologist, Part 1   21

The Cultural Anthropologist, Part 2   23

The Curator   25

The Weather   27

The Register   28

The Luxury Consultant   29

The Forensics Team   32

The Municipal Landscaper   33

The Framer   35

The Internist   37

The Rider   39

The Concierge   41

The Correspondent   43

The Radio Producer   44

The Florist   46

The Diplomat   48

The Journalist   49

The Forensics Team   51

The Twins   52

The Stenographer   55

The Ingenue   56

The Centaur   58

The Collector   61

The Copy Editor   62

The Runner   64

The Actuary   65

The Dancer   67

The Makeup Counter   68

The Blogger   69

The Talking Heads   71

The Housekeeper   73

The Adjunct   74

The Forensics Team   76

The Provost   77

The Dreamboat   78

The Teller   80

The Shopper   82

The Temp   83

The Tour Guide   84

The Neotranscendentalist   85

The Forensics Team   87

The Designer   88

The Nostalgist   90

The Cops   92

The Impalement Artist   93

The Transplant   95

The Pollster   97

The Forensics Team   100

The Industrial Architect   101

The Narc   103

The Third Shift   105

The Cartographer   107

The Backpacker   109

The Forensics Team   111

The Groundskeeper   112

The Opening Act   113

The Visitor in the Hills   114

The Crone   115

The Misanthrope   119

The Ringmaster   122

The Gardener   124

The Forensics Team   125

The Detective   126

Acknowledgments   131

LONER FORENSICS

HEAD SOUTH, CATAFALQUE

[ ]

All silence cedes to an era's loss, and
in ceding, withdraws its single
comfort like night through the
upended city. Up cobbled rises, past
branded stone and bridges, time
points receding over the harbor,
through the desert, into forested hills
surrounding. Ravines teem, unlikely
critters in the city's vaults, given
space passed over, under arches.
The silence does not drown, glazing
where it courses, away-glow of let-go
across the dewy blades of every park.

[ ]

In single rooms, in a field, afloat, in
the street, a shop, empty lots,
the hotel, on-screen, their shadows
still warm, disappeared, subsumed in
expanding humid noise, each
other's hazy limbs.

[ ]

Up the way, an inner-office parlor
where ghosts crowd umber settees,
dewing flowered ceramics, fluttering
paper streamers stuck from air vents,

red crepe or punctured orchid petals
strung like popcorn, compressed
gasses, spectral guesses at what's
altered. Before you, a crystal cracks,
the overhead sputters as they merge,
ascending, draining the room
of its proto-investigatory aurora.

[ ]
Outside, after the call, before
the silence you would be meeting you
there by this night's crumbling
fountain, floating through these,
the city's off-hours, repurposed. Off-
gassed mist brightening as chattering
recolonizes air, levitates about
the clear pool, hovers like a glass
shell, visitors drawn by instinct,
ghosts, trickle, and stone. The square
empty, cobble damp,
swamp green
light and rock.

] [

[ ]
You're always saying you've seen
things you can't explain, but you can

explain them: they're people, their
ghosts. Sorry, they're you, these
shadowy disturbances, mirthless
scuttling, endless toasts, celebratory
tents lined loosely with bulbs, their
flashes, dance floors, their weddings
and promotions and retirements,
their diminishments, their receding
heat. Goes without saying.

[ ]
And oh my, oh, limitless tender pretty
skepticism: what a way to further
your trademark resilience, branded
memory, assembling a simple red
wreath on a gray apartment door
signaling steadfast mourning,
a partner's disappearance, a fault
in the procedure so many years in
its creation. So many boxes ticked
and for what? Now the ramble, where
to look for guilt or conviction, or
remember the city reabsorbs
recognition shock into dark bars and
pulses, then peachy daybreak forever
breaking forever breaking in.

[ ]
To be re-questioned, requisitioned,
by that same you peering at you

around the far corner of your
darkened office hallway, power cut,
then doubled over your cubicle wall,
red eyes fixed and an indoor palm
and an ochre thread from portrait to
portrait and a haze from the vents
and a staircase materialized
from starlight in every flash
and rumble of smoke.

[ ]

And what about all these endlessly
recurrent visions, excessive,
recursive, successive execution
meaning what in the face of new
disappearance? Even a shining shock,
foretold, even the aura's luster-facing
umbra, facing stalling wonder, stuck
in place as with a pin, run cleanly
through. Even nothing but the dull
smell of dust around the catafalques,
erected outdoors on the park paths
at night, flanked by
columns of city steam.

] [

[ ]
The silence recedes like nothing
disruptive, like a silver thread pulls
through a storm of whistles and bells
and wildlife, branches, rattling, sway
and chatter, edging sky ice cracks and
falling pieces by pieces to the city,
and the light from everywhere
unendingly refracted, feeds brilliancy
back to the eye, only partial to
the breeze when gifted capital
thwarts keener discomfort.

[ ]
What then? Recall security
as reckless borders,
divisions made gravitational
by heat. You know it, you don't, you
do. A folding telescope left on the sill
in the empty apartment pointed to
the window in brick across the way,
bronze worried to shine, and still you
know it, you know it, you do.

] [

[ ]

Now outdoors, you know it, you do:
over the mountain must come
lumbering that fur-and-fleas, mass
made sturdy by movement
and volatile. In the face of it, breath
huffs, steam floats for a moment then
darkens and falls, shatters, black
shards shining in the cold, leaving
the land's brush to draw blood
from comers down the line, backed
up beyond the rise,
waiting, snorting, scratching.

[ ]

Why such necessity? Why drawing
a steady path, slow incline, why
gesture, brow raised, why all that
darkness, viscid, waiting in the wings
to hulk up over the mountain, across
the desert, down the valley, toward,
toward, stench like tar and hide, new
earth. The mountain shrugs, resettles,
and still they appear.

] [

[ ]

And   so,   upon   release
from the briefing, it's hard to see
that circling helicopter as anything
other than your own absent heart,
spiriting across the darkened city
searching   rooftops,   alleyways,
for evidence, something as simple
as a winter flower, a regional vision,
thumping   air   and   roving   beam,
window   through   the   residual
clamor   and   fog.

[ ]

What a parlor game, you used to say
to you, waiting for a lift. To stand
on   the   curb,   on   the   stone   steps
of   the   monument,   the   fountain,
the city altar, tracking rising light,
silence   receding   up   limestone
and brick. To   take   up   regular
temporary residence in every hospital
ever built. To have brought oneself to
depths of weightlessness approaching
true investigation. A lie? What a hoot,
you'd say and raise your glass to you
who couldn't watch. Plastic in the life
support's glow and bleats, and what

does it mean to have been
brought here to spectate, all
your suited fellows watching
and breathing and silent, respectful.

[ ]
And what does the hand that directs
the viewing support through
its gestures? Gentle guidance of
the chin toward constellations
through leaves. Systematic. What
structures of endgames, what
structures of stopgaps, stopping
gape?   Everywhere,
a tired resistance, retiring.

] [

[ ]
Nose to black wall back in the office,
windows grown over as the volume
now rises from outside,
mockingbirds, car alarms, a carnival,
motorbikes screaming around
a Globe of Death. The brutal sun.
The wall quivers then holds, quivers
then cracks then compresses. Ridges

and valleys crumble into shape but
your perspective, captive, allows little
recognition of tectonics beyond
the smell that seeps from the effort:
cinnamon, shit, cedar, animal.

] [

[ ]

A bell tower centers the glaring city,
beacon for ghosts stirring through.
What etiquette, reflection? Some
disappearance and the parks grow on,
filling skeletal vacants with new
cycling sprouts, hopeful in a last
warm gasp. All seasons at once, daily,
nightly, the silence, the noise.

[ ]

A profile, a game, a portrait
and thrills. Lush and still, electronic
underpinning rumble. Humming,
your hair catches the flame of
the devotional candle in front of you,
Detective, you are unharmed, but
to what end. And now the smell of
black tea and anise, and later subtle

snow   falls,   catching   only
the   streetlights'   sodium
pillars   before   evaporating.

[ ]
The department, shuttered, parlors,
shuttered, office, ringing, memory,
exit, whisked to the Forensics Lab.
The residual silence turns watery,
was already watery. The ghosts turn
watery, were already watery, run
down the walls and storm drains.
Silver threads their work. Turning
to close, you and you know it
and   expect   it,   and
always   reliability   accomplishes
nothing   but   slow   submersion.

[ ]
Disappearances, and we know no
other   way   to   live.

[ ]
Constant production, and we know no
other   way   to   live.

] [

[The interviews that follow]   [the city
that follows]   [the interviews of]
[the dream where]   [the answer
to]   [the city of]   [the time when]
[the figment who]   [the story
stalled]   [the you is]   [the you is]
[the you is]   [the wrong way]
[to   go]   [about   this]

THE ANNOTATOR

[The dream where] [The world where] [The city where] The light comes through the waking night window golden, then blue, then violet, each its own mood, [demarcation of] wellness, life, uncertainty in the absent animals one loves, [asleep,] whirring. Blue then rose, a cruiser menacingly lit up and silent down the alleyway [below the frame], night birds feeding all hours, seeds falling, tapping the sill, golden then blue [separated by] fitful, by more dreams, a beast sulking away down the dashed white of the street, best chances, wet pavement, [clicks, a stirring,] some Weather. But not a dream. Something less permanent but not quite; the city, its own dream, dreams of itself, repeated in a crescent for [a time,] an irregular pendulum, until, passing, we, inhabitants, wake.

THE FORENSICS TEAM

[In this stalled instance]

The Forensics Team gathers, alights, disperses, regroups, arcs, examines all the avenues by which it might take further flight. Examines the Weather, the signs, the prints, for plot. Finds [REDACTED]

Here, abrasion. That one, powdery substance. Team members won't speak for themselves, refusing interviews.

THE MAYOR

What was your question? My official
statement: a single sprouted leaf on
the stem of a withered orchid, each idea
emerges and decomposes quickly into
something a lot like nothing. Like this
rolling, disorienting fog through my tall
city. First the monument tops, looming
historical   wartime   figures
absent   their   heads,

their swords, human property, off-kilter,
then   the   bottoms   of   buildings   so
the sleeping stories up hover without
knowing   [the   dream   where]:
overwhelming   geranium,   hyacinth,
incense   just   this   side   of   rot,
unmistakable,   the   hotel   lobby   facing
the greening fountain. The Concierge
all   aglow   from   it.

I've   rallied   the   public,   pleaded
for   patience.   Still,   Forensics   wants
an avenue, a series, data points, a sterile
process. If I've learned anything, this
mist   can   whiff   nightsweet,   can   you
remember? [Do you] won't they, will,
worry,   wait,   come   back.

It never rains near the mayoral mansion,
and   that   meaning   obliterates.   Order
the   slush   shoveled   from   ditch   to   dry
ground,   call   the   Gardener,   and

new   flowers   every   day—sharp
white,   small   mint,   cat   purple,   vote
yellow,   road-shoulder   pink.

Forensics can record, can remember,
same   diff,   derive,   rule   out.   Is   it
the grasses that memorize our two-step,
Detective?   Absent   lazy   who: stop
harming. They say the city brought on
the   disappearances,   but   me,   I   see
new   space   for   an   imaginary   condo
complex   I   unquestioningly   support.

No one question but a few, like we'll
dismantle   each   other   asking   favors,
yachts,   my   unnecessary,   undesired
etiquette, still blue-blue, still beautiful in
the right light, which follows me—my
everywhere,   my   colossal   meteor—I'm
sure of it. But keep looking, Detective.

Leave   a   message.

THE PALM READER

Are you following your nose? [Hint: The story is a dream.] This is
more   of   a   story—you   are   [not].

Are   you   able   to   understand   it?   You   don't   want   your
investigation   burdened   by   moods.   The   you
were   there.   And   you.

Into this scene you place you, you place your voice, your
number-one voice, your voice assertive in Monday morning
meetings, at the center, as the solder, as a canvas and
the   framing,   the   gesso,   as   the   oils,   the   brushes,
the   reproductions,   as   the   whole   sticky   shebang.

[Hint: This   instance   is   stalled,   is   a   song.]

I mean to say I don't miss myself before the silences cut
through by bells, but then sometimes, just barely, I hear music
outside, down the avenue. And it's like—it's like your life seals
up, for those minutes, into an underwater room of dark blues
and velvet reds, amniotic, maybe, but more like space.
Hurtling that's more like stasis. The comfort of it, the never
going back. I was different in the center of me, did I [you did].
More   brittle,   a   moss   or   crystalline   biome.

In   that   hurtling,   things   are   okay.

[Hint: The   dream   is   not   a   puzzle.]

But you. Why do you arrive making such sad sounds?

It's   true: no   one   ever   knows   when
you   love   them—no   one   could.

But everyone. You, listen: everyone knows something's afoot.

THE AMATEURS

Coercing the Palm Reader the day the mountains darken, we all prepare with methods most us: baroque boxes of many consumer   materials,   foils,   lenses   bought and   branded,   and   some with   nothing—a   squint.

We look to the sky in stranger clusters, curious, unsure, and the birds keep eating seed from the suet feeder affixed to the fire escape, tapping, light clatter, the cat sleeps, curled. None of the prophesied evidence becomes. The sky darkens like   a   storm   above   the   bell   tower even   as   a   real   storm   [the   ghost   who]   worries the periphery, flashing to the west. Elsewhere, a dusk glows from   all   approaches   to   horizon,   encircling,   holding   fast despite   some   who   journeyed   up   to   watch   it bend   to   sphere.

A central darkness, smothered light. The Gardener lays hands on   a   sapling,   leaves   quake.   A   dark   like   our   silences   but none   of   it   ungraspable.   So   much   time   between   this and   the   next,   to   prepare or   send   it   out   of   our   minds.   Not   like   here. Quaver,   no—shadows   lift

and   pull   apart,   and   we   go back   to   our   regular   business.

All those observers out there, you might think the silence of no people is just a different kind of organic noise, but usually the silence of no people is just silence, obliterating. Nothing else interpretable, and what to call that fleeting state of deprivation? All the city, a night bird's call—all the city collapsed. Harbor swollen from a storm: it's too easy to dip a toe and forget existentialism, never mind a fun thought experiment in the rain, singing round a lamppost.

I see inconsistent environmental events and regional turns of phrase. The Curator can explain:

Some of these people, [the dream where] some of them, they're in love.

You don't just stop singing when you're in that golden-hour natural light of municipal fear, for fear, by fear.

What   was   the   question?

I'm too internet to be mystical and yet. Who wants to explain
the development's momentum, monument to mangled efficiency,
a healthy work-utopia balance. Well-appointed apartments append
the commuter train, the altar.

Endlessly scrolling through my research, I don't want to take a walk or work,
but I would accept cash at my temporary threshold, evidence of care
provided by the management, all thresholds being temporary, and all money
a perfect summer night: just a little muggy, enough to keep everyone awake
and roaming the streets but quietly, without purpose.
Hold on a sec [TEMPORARILY DISCONNECTED]

[RECONNECTED] I meant to tell you: a cruiser rolls by, lights spinning lazily silent. Observant oppressive or too tired to. I keep wishing, with all my mustered love, for cash—my goodness—yet none appears.

I mean, certain segments of our population in the desert recreational areas have established efficient enough support systems such that being outdoors willingly, for long periods of time, ultimately requires the management of profound, transformative boredom, and how is this possible? We've come so far. The Mayor says so in her briefings.

Me? I will discover the reason for the rich, the sun, the temporary, sulking dark.

I mean it: some of these people are in love.

We've come so far.

And the rich,

they'll disappear. never

24

THE CURATOR

Connection like a natural thing, diminishing. Who sent you?

Returns on, *turns on* good or bad depending on where the *you* is;   stand   closer,   this   art'll   [   ].

Stand   closer,   touch   stealthily.
Stand   closer,   flip   the   camera.

You, like copper wires in sheaves from ceiling to industrial cement   floor,   spotlit   artifactually   and   cosmic.

If you trace ideas on the adjacent wall with just enough destabilization evidenced through novel text placement, incompletion, sans serif, detour, is that closer to feeling a feeling than turning around and feeling something different through   self-removal?   See   for   yourself:

] [

Precision edges dismantlement, but institutionally situated and   therefore   contained.
The   Framer   keeps   framing   thinly,   ever
thinner,   requests   payment.

And what if you actually get a kick out of it, tho? Dismantlement? Curses. What if you hate documentation and have no theories about it, but you know what's going on outside   your   work,   the   city   is   [   ].

Why a point, an original conclusion one hardly gets to and is
never   expected   to   keep   past   the   next   installation:
a   starry   sky   in   the   desert.

There's nothing alive inside this gallery, and that's the way
I like it. The Ingenue snapping selfies in the exhibition
green zone. Illusion instead of escape. Escape, to display it,
an exhaustion born of various deficiencies I don't have
the   heart   to   document.   Keep   studying   to   what   edge,
an   end   maybe.   But
to   a   depth—sure.

Look   here.   Sounds   right.

THE WEATHER

Autumn one late rain-dark all lingering water pulled heavy to the ground. Familiar and rundown hill to harbor so later rising light meets air conscience cleared, simple fix, fizz or one easy air is pleasure wrung out, is all morning was yellower, recasting local hotel gutted brick. To be recast like a film clear pressed just, scrolled, pushed up black nail crescent crests above the bed, pink above the finger pad, that easy ominous oval, a warning point.

[Don't come here,] change your life.

Exchange for gothic, some deader. But hovering at the cornerstone, bluish metal finally cooled overnight, blush swamp receded, dry, one pleasure before the heat dome recloses, smothers rising dusky, steamy sleeping in the park then, before morning.

The every-heron settles across the way on a detached pier overgrown with grasses and goldenrod and streaks of rot, stands still in institutionalized mini-island limbo. Such a willful little park with fisher bird, cut off like an inaccessible idea rooted floating, rooted inaccessible, and a name, a reason, a word: I love you, you are safe.

Honestly, there's a lot of time killing. I'm tired of feeling
powerful   from   it.

In this city, the city disappears people invisibly until we are
the   city,   and   we   are
already the city. Or, visibly but immediately institutionally
recast invisible. Not immediately immediately; more
like eventually immediately. Gaslit, the self-
help internet says, newly neatly lowercased to better fit in
among our endless redundant electronic affirmations.
Heal yourself on your off-hours, unrecorded,
and   post   the   results.   Tally.
The city quietly recognizes itself around the fog
creeping,   and   we   are   the   city.

Once a shift, I visit the Teller in her smart cage for change.
The Palm Reader comes in for quarters. The Actuary
intones, moans, can't make a decision. [The story where]
the structure's inevitable, checking IDs, collecting covers,
in kind, no change. Reorganized. Citizens buying Taquitos
all hours of the day and night. Okay. Reconfigured attention.
What was the question? I've been waiting long
enough   to   keep   watching   it   happen.

[Welcome,] click. Just so for snaps, I'll describe your message's psychodynamic constitution as lacking follow-through, though for now I'll respond from this tropical sailboat where I am anymore half the time. Can you hear me? My connection [TEMPORARILY DISCONNECTED]

[RECONNECTED] I left. Anyone can be, too:

choose comfort, cream, metaphorically fat living, like sleeping excessively in, an ooey-gooey live stream, heart-filtered. Choose thread count by adherence to steady ambient light levels, modified vibraphone awakenings designed for each new dawn, volume, equalizer ping, and here goes another shelf of turquoise water careening into mist off the bow. [The city where] I used to know rain by tires gushing on endless alleys, and another pass, each new potion conjuring a pastel memory, softening what ought to be a bitter spell.

Now, I find fancy furniture affixed to the floorboards, blister packs spent before bedtime, bottomless per diem, cut and tightening of the skin of the throat. My Internist visits the ship, elides actionable offense, eats oysters.

I felt good answering your interview request, Detective, because nothing should be so easy, like reposting someone else's art with a smiling cat emoji [the city is not].

I can't say I'm directly affected when I'm the cause—all I've let slide.

[The   dream   is   a   song   is   not]

[TEMPORARILY   DISCONNECTED   RECONNECTED]

Sunk charms dulled and resurfaced: an amethyst, a self-investigation, a bloodstone, sunstone, heliotrope, a checking-in image spared, emerald incantation about a heartbeat, heart-center, exorcised, carrying one through one's day, as though benevolence, a commodity.

Yes, technically I'm an expat.

Already or still fatigue takes root and spreads, affixes, multiplies. The boredoms are all different, monotonous novelty, marvelous distraction, my for-now home, afloat, bedrooms all variously adorned, distracted thematic. I've drowned the captain's log decoratively, a long tether to shore.

THE FORENSICS TEAM

[In this interview]

A cold apartment. The Forensics Team—ribbony, flitting—wants
to make you a cup of tea, care, dumbed, about how you came to
never exist in the city both before and after you came into it.
Sorry   for   your   [   ].   Thoughts   and   [   ].

THE MUNICIPAL LANDSCAPER

I can't work through this heat,
the Weather, drips smudge ink,
like haven't we, O me, already
solved this inconvenience
with an infallible ink, its marks true
blue? My troubled swamp, a lowland
in fountain spray even in ghostly
rain—a mist. Someone singing
in the bell tower, everything I do
for the taste of it.

Please report this
information to the Mayor:

Inefficiency, cut field grasses
repurposed in the city center. Another
heat dome closes, years pass. I stop
submitting to the heat, which means I
begin to submit without forethought:
a simple decision. A scorching, runny
kind of heat. Thick and thinking
slowly. Rot around the roots.

Out in the desert surrounding
the city, a sandstone castle rises
with life. A whole city unto itself,
spiraling graciously up
like the folds of an immense gown.
Lavish, populated, pristine.
I've stopped spelling, casting.

Outside, the Runner keeps circling
the growth, follows the paths
established, energy bars, electrolytes
parachuted from heaven's helicopters.
I imagine this place as
I've heard it's true.

Here, green and formstone.
Some glass, some garbage, and work.
The city leads. Into the mouth
of a buttercup; flowers
here despite the heat.

THE FRAMER

Though my hours are lately critically curtailed, my purpose stills: framing perspective such that the brain does not become confused, the depth just trickery but enough for discussion, for proxy, for progress.

See the frame, heavy in inception, thin over time, finally disappearing replaced by full-bleed. In digital and print. There is still potential for confusion, we just no longer care, welcome the mismatch, the brain registering depth where there is none. Did the Curator send you, send instructions, send payment?

[The frame is not]

What's the difference between a flat image depicting depth and depth itself if the viewer will never travel toward it. Knock knock. Empiricism. You will close your eyes, and I am you today. I will close my eyes and step back and turn. I will watch the blood move across my eyelids, facing a bright window, and know that it is yours. The blood. A fiber-optic crepe between us, Detective.

[The dream is not a clue]

This frame enclosing not a landscape but an image of the landscape as appears from inside. The city shimmers today past the sill and aftermath. Wiry streaks of light and lighter smudges carry across, more a field of orange pekoe plaster, my wall. Where have the disappeared gone? Where are their spotlit sheaves of copper wire? To travel toward, dearth of faith in representation, doing the work for us.

A blue-gray sunrise through the shutters. I have nothing to. I have an idea of the symptoms.

Inside where I live are teas for all occasions, the same occasion repeated irregularly. Remember when being sad or sick was sad or regrettable? Now, I take a sick day to feel free for a few hours. I feel still, still feel. I have an idea this is nothing to share. I slip from frank to bitter. It's an easy slip. I touch patients gingerly with my elbows. What brings you [are you there]?

I watch the unexpected snowfall, and I see nothing. I watch the unexpected snow fall through the municipal streetlights, and I see a city bus, red and air brakes, the Pink Line crosstown, and I see a bundled figure lifting an umbrella on the corner as the bus huffs by. I watch unexpected spring in the greenish gaps, and I feel like I ought to keep watching, to witness and then what. I imagine a sailboat in the tropics, been there, I feel, can you imagine. Understand? The Luxury Consultant's delicate foreign fruits.

It's not quieter. Though it's said the snow makes a city quieter; it doesn't. The ground is warm. The slush and wheels. [The dream where] I remember the rural snow quiet and how I shouldn't share it. Not like that, like how everybody already knows it's not amber or fluorescent, just dark and the darker edges of the forest bled in closer, maybe rustle as a drift falls from a bough. An owl up there. You can't see anything coming toward you:

] [

You can't see everything coming toward you. And it is. Figures you know kissing under the owl, and only you know it's there, feathers like bark: changeable. Here, the city is excited by the Weather, sliding and smiling and yelling disrupted expectation. A relief, a diversion, empty patches of ground all uniform for a minute, everything capacity, full, unsilent. I see nothing. Stops when you look up, silence coming toward you. Realize now. You've receded into memory.

THE RIDER

What's   my
presence?   You're
asking,   Detective,
if I'm hungry, is my
hunger   broad?
Alert?   Self-search
for a quiet place,
brighter, everdawn,
secured.   Outside
this   municipal
transportation,   an
alarm   and   alarm
and   alarm   until
nothing's   noise
folds   in   again,
edges smoothed, a
familiar   haunted
limb. View through
the   window   a
tearable   reel   of
formstone,
formstone,
storefront,   tree,
eyes from behind it
all,   watery.
A raised umbrella.
Silent   sliver
vanishingly
narrow, alerted, a
slice   heavenly
isolated   until
believably singular,

truth folds in a dark
shutoff, warmed
damaging corona,
sterile. Safer, then.
A helpless control,
control unpeopled,
no wonder it's so
difficult to imagine
midflight.

THE CONCIERGE

Personalities in and out,
fading or walking,
taking in the lobby
with its marble columns,
brass accents, massive
bouquets of snapdragon,
bird of paradise,
lily, refreshed
biweekly, nonnative,
locally sourced, trashed.

[ ]

I provide maps
and guidebooks, offer
coffee or a polished
apple. Premium rooms
stocked with
complimentary ghosts or
holograms of
the recently vanished
to greet their temporary
occupants, love them,

tend to them, offer up
the contents of
the minibar, lament
the city sympathetically,
tour them around
the sights with a song,
a stun gun, five-star
online reviews, every
one. Locals wandering
past the chain-link

Staying or paying
visits, occupancy ebbs
and recovers, which I
am, possessed of, into or
out of each room's
decorative elements
and heavy-framed
mirrors. Out-of-town
entrepreneur, the
Mayor's entourage,

professional baseball
team: I imagine
them their needs
before them, set out
like cutlery
at a banquet. And so I
am or become and
remain myself:
a literal, quaint,
question of a person.

patio see new
as a list of remember
-when, a place
warmed under
the glow still
unacknowledged, a full
home until
a certain segment
claims it through
schematized ubiquity.

[ ]

A wet city, humid
with a harbor teasing
visitors to leave the
municipality, continue
toward the sea, the
desert, its ghosts,

to take a stand, to
disavow my employers,
their gloomy bar
-lounge from where
the Diplomat's been
lately missing, indoor

pool planted round
with tropicals in local soil,
always ready. I
welcome some back.
The rotation becomes
me, my concern.

THE CORRESPONDENT

All day all I think is I'm tired and typing, ticker. Telling stories, this story, over and. Still, stalled. Am I talking too much or for. And why a girlish void person of emotional scaffolding a demon, a deadness. A depth, non-romantic. As though. The real disappearances front-paged and swallowed. As told by the Journalist, who just. Tells.

I report as best I [TEMPORARILY DISCONNECTED] the Talking Heads' wide-eyed rebuttal.

[ ]
[RECONNECTED] The desert a lesser ecosystem than forest. Nah. Maybe decadent, the hierarchy, regressive gender. The hysterics of my forebears have worn me down. I report, again, saddened. Can you provide a quote, something actionable.

[ ] holler.

As if to pretend there's been a change in element rather than reportage. Team sports is. [If and the city is] living without a reveal, building toward Help-Me TV, where I plead into the color gels: I'd like a social system I can join but privately, without leaving me, my screenshots, my clips, broadcast dish to dish through the city [is not a].

[ ]
Help-Me TV, I feel, I feel I'm so tired despite my scheduled recuperation. What's been happening here? Am I talking to too many people or for. Am I so much or too I. Is it all this tedious, these climates, this grasping, that coverage, those retractions. To push forth and pull back analyzed data, fog, brain to eye-brain to brain. Sexy, but not the aspirational kind. This quiet, you, this quiet, I hate to fill it.

Dear listener, dear Detective, I don't know what you want from your dead decade, but I still can't dance, and my horoscope's a mess.

No true summer jam for five years and counting, the city in a cyclical hunker, pools closed, and not only for the lack. Ten years? Sound fashion in a clave loop, laser-y and tropicalia. We're ducking, sitting, sweating in a metallic summer haze that'll only grow into its true purpose once nostalgia simmers up, in other words. Soon. When the Weather turns. Late leaves still middle green.

I walk, spiral out from my curbed personal city center in swelling squares until the grid breaks down, humidity killing the motor, sparks of progress, conversation. Past an unexpectedly crowded lot, a congregation: the Gardener cradles a sapling. Street-level weeds, chip bags, the bowed bottom steps of marble stoops.

Every night the row homes glow a little; empty car dealership, empty strip mall, empty check cashing, empty carry-out. The night fog comes on. My spiral, clockwise or counter, counters me, my hunker, ready for sway,

a breeze even. Moving for the sound of it. Because we're expected to.
What was your question? I've heard what I'm told.

THE FLORIST

[Shutters up] when I take my prescriptions, I halve them carefully with the edge of a slanted tweezer blade. Call this predictable; I call it intimate. I can almost imagine myself a florist. I can almost immediately imagine myself an intimate florist, in a shop no one visits, down a curving cobbled street. It's dark. There are golden lamps. My vista windows soon to frame an alley instead of the red and silver daytime skyline, Self says. Maybe a dumpster or a laundry vent. It's dark, and I can only ever taste the inside of my mouth, ashy and uninviting.

I woke up dead yesterday over daytime email, but do I? Self said, I'm right here standing at my workstation like I always have to do.

The sky like tissue paper, landscape a tearable reel of brownstone, brownstone, hospital, tree, glare from behind it all, watery. The Concierge orders bouquets, exotics. Self says, I am a direct dismissal of an animal at work, excused exclusively by teeth. I miss my partner when they're at work and I'm at work.

I think, There are so many altos and so many instrumentals and instructional videos of them all.

I feel like [the dream is]

I finger the carnations. I push the baby's breath behind my ears. I watch out the diminishing window for   someone,   tonight,   to   come   by.

THE DIPLOMAT

Have a seat. Have you noticed how the sun closes in outside the city? Or the land lower down supports its own protections: humidity, shade. Embracing heat, days of the low landscape presses in unwanted—same—but doesn't pummel. A wilted church banner discloses: no one should ever acquiesce to be touched by others, even as the holidays burn on. Bleached ghost town administered by the city, a place to exercise my immunity. The Mayor won't learn basic protocol.

[ ]

The buses run wildly so, but still there are some buses.

[ ]

On the surface, everyone's defensive. The Mayor's lost interest in her friends. No one buys me drinks anymore when I slide my business card across a dark bar. Intelligence tradecraft. Code words for embargos, a feel-good argument. Still I write everything down. [The city is] like I said, the Mayor's lost interest in gathering intelligence, mine, gathering me up in her arms, stroking my notepad, my pen. Wrong or incomplete, friends all rich gossips, but lately I think they've gotten wise, grown cold. No new messages. No more meetings in alleyways or on bus benches with newspapers or coffees, like passing the time in places they've never been. It's okay though. Now, I feed the coyotes—same—I recall the greening fountain outside—same—her protection seemed promising when I began, like a well-earned bludgeoning. I lounged on her yacht deck. A secured, well-ventilated space. I know better now. Now, the sometime silences all around the mansion. And I know it's time to begin listening in earnest.

THE JOURNALIST

[NOTES:] [The song is not a dream] Where the you is,   Detective,   you   wanted   [REDACTED]

Out   their   window   [REDACTED]   hears some   constellation:

Cluster like echinacea in a vacant lot, single willow, torn   canvas   all   about   a   first-murky   mood summoned for answers, whining cicada, view from the   stoops   a   galaxy   forming.

The   crowd   condenses,   kneeling,   sweating, bubbling,   warding   off   evil   interference with   righteous   action.   Sun   sets, fog   passes,   a   looming projection,   quick   refocus.

[REDACTED]   peers,   spies   the   Twins   illuminated, enlisted   to   summon   investigatory   demons from the   dimming   gold-pink   air,   irises   around the   chain-link,   nonnative   grasses, the   solidifying   congregation.

Enacted   spectral   petitioning,   emerald   in-line emissions of their,   our,   their   gem-strong   chests unencumbered,   spilling   light,   a   breath, [REDACTED]   too   takes   notes.

Amid   some   burble,   the   Twins   begin:

[START FIELD RECORDING]

We want you to   Feel something
We want you to   Feel something

Familiar, unnamable, drowning in interacting with
this our landscape, this our story, this [the city is]
our web series, our docudrama, clicks-for-likes,
send   help   to   those   who   need   it.

[END FIELD RECORDING]

As   seen   and   documented   by   [REDACTED],
the Twins crouch, red knuckles to feet, to grass,
crouching,   the   crowd   crouches,   closes   in,
the   demons   low-rustle   through
the city behind them like a searching breeze,

loyal   as   dogs   heeling.

THE FORENSICS TEAM

[In this scene]

They [the you is] chirp:

What if we never leave again

What if the city exists to shut you out

What if all this is yours

THE TWINS

[START FIELD RECORDING]

Like a breeze, our demons
Loyal as dogs

Heeling, our summoning
Our summoning brings

A peach to the party
A beach to the city, a calm

To the waters that lap at
Our braids, our tongues we bow to

The harbor, we face the desert
We've moved farther from

The lot where we found
The impression where flowers

Of the first, we have found
More, more in light filtered

Blue through aquarium
Tanks, slow sharks and rays

And divers, low-pile carpet to quiet
Still singing, we hear we

Hear, our demons help
Search, speak only to each other

Despite interview requests, entreaties
From the system to help

We help or are we
Point past, have

Sharpened our focus, our
Focal radical we

Grant none, we post, we
Continue our play, our ask

Bring only ourselves as
The music swells, the LEDs

Stream from mast to flagpole
Flagpole to lamppost

And at night the city
Returns to trace

Its vessel paths through re-
Ceded silence, still

Sticky with damp [we see
It] with slick with sick with

What remains on our tongue
Tongues everything altered

As usual, lights
Drip up drip down brick

Across dirt hauled in
For arrangement, mulch hauled

And the Gardener watches us
Crouched behind the willow

Approximate decay-stalling
Annuals and lush in rest before

Brownstones, we search, search
Listen, channel, project

Does public beautification face
Its violence, institutional

Light aim, aims
True through each who calls

To it, calls to it to frighten it
Away, heeling

[END FIELD RECORDING]

THE STENOGRAPHER

the   sky   is   breaking
apart [   ] it's full of
mockingbirds,   I
dream   [   ]   like
whirlpools,   gyres,   a
twister,   a   snail,   a
braid   of   amber   hair
unraveling [   ] if I [   ]
knew   better,   I'd
name   these   spins
my maker [   ] a shell
only [   ] my taste, a
shame [   ] I'm all for
easy   [   ]   we   can
clutter   up   our   ethics
investigation,   sure   [
] make it simple with
flotsam   [   ]   quiet
women   spilling   their
tales   to   the
chairman's
undersecretary's
assistant's   cousin's
gig-economy   intern's
company-issued
smartphone's   voice
transcription app [   ]
for the record [   ] tell
a joke for [   ] the
record [for the city]
and   kill   it   [   ]
every   time

THE INGENUE

After months of light living,
vitamin deficiency.

My nails peel, and I do nothing.
Maybe yoga. Feathered
peacock pose.

Anemia, nothing. My opinion?
Your question. I spill.

Glass shag, flags up, nothing, but I
do cringe secretly, my augmented
sold Self, my invisible benefits'
promised reality gestures. My live-
work studio with galley kitchen.

It's all in the lighting, head forward
and slightly down. Grateful. Toss
up reality in joyful, polleny fields
to clogged mortal portals. Okay to
sell now, okay concatenated
crackles, the morals of it.

Here, at this moment, I want to
talk about my failures sarcastically,
systematically, threateningly,
profitably, but my taste inevitably
sours, or failure unregisters,
unfollows. These starlings
everywhere about you. [Did you
expect me here, didn't you]

Failure to engage in the city, my city, where the lighting is poor. Very gendered. An overexposed photo of oatmeal and flaxseed. You understand. I explained this all to the Visitor before they packed their pens and left, who nodded.

Culture works for me to tack onto or, TFW, become in the middle of, if only. To derive, sell, a dense melon-death-pink cloud like tulle all about the face, a person ensconced and beloved by others so like them.

I see my cloud, sturdy my crystalline frames, sell honey infused with hyaluronic acid.

I venture out into the noise, edgy bells from the tower, distant, and a green mist surrounds the monument's base. The Curator extends her palm. I photograph, post from the waist up. Keep it simple. I am in control of this fog. We are the same.

The Radio Producer says, Clean coal technology, we cannot be handy. If what the Correspondent says is any indication, celebrations and rallies: a true-blue legacy in celebrity spokespersonship, money for the cause. I believe art can be conceptual, but at what cost? I'm so tired, but I can still talk about it, so there's that.

I believe in the regional environment, flooding with unmined coal, the Radio Producer pronounces, How can the city's population, shrinking. How can I become accessible, says the Centaur. I deserve it: the accolades, jealous disdain. I work, see? I'm so tired from it. How can I become the accessible me I deserve to be, all the attributes I deserve to inhabit or be bestowed with, says the garland around the waist of the Centaur. But which waste? How can I become accessible, a port, writing, a human.

How accessible can becoming such a cost. Is it time yet? Maybe it's not time yet. I'd like to tell a story. I'd like to start telling a story. I'm starting to like to tell a story: wanting. But how to become a person, accessible. Cost worthy, a fee in advance of my personality. A portal.

I can access information, news even. The Correspondent understands. I know what's happening even when it's not happening to me, but it is. I live here. I mean, who knows, but easy does it, Detective.

For you, I will ask my rich friends, who will ask their rich friends, who will buy me a boat, most luxurious of hobbies. The yacht of a foreign oligarch spotted parked next to the Mayor's rich friend's yacht in the tropics, as reported by the Correspondent, who understands. What's on the warm inside but place settings, gold rimmed, crystal goblets, smoked fish, vitamin supplements, vast oceans of food. Like a cruise ship, but meted out in smaller portions to fewer people and therefore classier: an identification, an acknowledgment accessible.

How can I become hungry enough, accessible. Strike that. Replace with, Who can I become unhungry enough to enjoy the taste of select foods in a small, distanced way. One never stops asking one's rich friend for a parking spot, a handshake, ranking position, penetration, glory, a garland of flowers. Call the Florist for repairs.

59

Ice melts and drips from the fire escape affixed to the front of the nineteenth-century double-wide brownstone where I rent a space to live. Let's not gussy this up.

It's not a tragedy, or it is, but it's a tragedy that sits on top of an easy disaster. Me? Sign me up. I can afford this headache for now.

THE COLLECTOR

I save a photo of my bed, unmade, on the home screen of my phone so I never forget from where I came. [Who are you again, again and] such is the extent of my domesticity: utter. The extent of me, most immediately as every morning snaps a new thread binding body to reflection. Is the reflection still who, flipped, unsettled in the city only as image. Lefts as rights, even the nearly symmetrical face becomes unsettling when reversed, like a delicate shift in cloud cover alters angles such that shadows become newly unfamiliar. The Framer sends a silver stream of selfies. Maybe that's what's happened. Why when I stumble across images of myself in someone else's record, a need to keep moving past. How it answers, that feed, too much at once.

THE COPY EDITOR

[SUBMITTED BY COURIER]

- Revise toward the style guide.
- Revise toward clarity and market forces.
- Revise toward the Weather, its moods.
- Revise toward reportage, the Journalist's ambition.
- Revise toward facts backed by silence statistics.
- ~~Revise toward fame.~~
- Revise toward a frame.
- Revise toward identifiable emotional residue coating a park bench.
- Revise toward a crick in the neck from looking back protectively.
- Revise toward a creepy week, repeated, weak and unloved, invisible in the news.
- Revise toward complete-protein breakfasts, lemon water at room temperature.
- ~~Revise toward shitting on a schedule, by force of a perfect will.~~
- And a Ouija board.
- Revise toward content, underpaid under production, perfected.
- Revive toward content, character, cryptography, the Stenographer's notes.
- Revise toward content, the rule of threes.
- And a permanent desk in [the dream is] a quiet office.
- Revise toward magnesium sleep, toward uninterrupted, toward uneventful waking, by force of a perfect will.
- A repeated dream state.
- Revise toward regular reenactment: all scenes, in reflection, off-silver-white to signal reappearances from the past.

[You know it, you do, this reappearance, as love.]
- Revise toward performance.
- And permanence.

- Revise toward redundancies, practicalities, a sharpened paring knife in a wooden block on the counter.
- Revise toward untamable visions born from a creepy week, repeated.
- ~~Revise toward how a poison process would be so slow, careful, tiny whirlpool in the tub.~~
- Revise toward fewer details, more mood.
- Revise toward getting succinct at the end, toward endless winking like a twitch, too loud a laugh to fit in one small apartment.
- Revise toward sunk to a sinking dark-sea floor.
- Stay there.

THE RUNNER

This morning I fell into the desert loop around the city carrying nothing, rare, expecting the act to feel liberating. Clumsy and carrying nothing but the heat, the direct sun of it. No cicada husks here, but some increase in chipmunks, silvery streaks through low brush. Near silence either reverent or apologetic, or probably I'm imagining things, those hulking figures summiting the far hills. Ask the Municipal Landscaper for an explanation, [the dream is not] a clue.

[The   city   is/is   not]   [The   time   when]

The wet city a mile east, metal and late meals, shade in the alleys, always one side of the street. Locust trees. Neighbors passing quietly below open windows, shutters, moving toward work or sleep in other indoor places. Now. I have stopped. I have turned toward home.

THE ACTUARY

You know, no one believes me when I say it, but this is the real me. [Thanks for asking,] I walk around myself a lot, spiraling toward the restroom in the other wing of the desert-friendly office park where I won't see these people I know. I walk myself around where I'm walking, tallying steps, where's a suitable corner for clinging into, an alter ego passing, the next pay grade up. What to calculate if someone's in distress in the hallway?

This is the real me [thanks for asking]: a bot; a radical recorded first in spare moments between assignments come through the project management solution, enterprise edition. No one believes me, no one believes unbelievable me, a steady static on the underside of the Talking Heads' giggling report. That's because it is. Too believable, who'd buy and forget already; this is the real me. In every sentence. I mean, assessing every sentence. Making an ass out of you and assuming.

I'm asserting myself through myself, [thanks for] working, for which I am paid. I'm red-lettering my asserting, my assessments, assets, numbered stages. I'm reading public domain books online during work hours. *Moby-Dick*. Goddamn, a whale between my figures! Moving around itself along searchable, believable routes. I could be anywhere, and I've chosen the desert recreational areas. The Talking Heads nod their approval. [Thank you,] a mindset bent on sending messages of assessment bent over.

Really, this is all about my walks to the company restroom. This me: real and persistent. Evergreen. The best parts of my day. If there's a you out there on the other end of my figuring, some old-fashioned sweeps for bugs, I see you, Detective.

I'm not a sad sack, exactly. More like a sad tote. The Temp and her Tupperware. What was your question?

Skeptical of too much everyday melancholy, or it's time for lunch or a snack; I can't tell what my body's telling me. Probably a sandwich and the same old sadness chasing after novelty that ends up more. These spirals getting nowhere or worse. The radio blares. You smile.

I'm tired of spacewalks, so many metals and mice sent up to live and be studied, reported on. When will it end? An asymptotic function, sympathetic. Suitable. Enough.

THE DANCER

I'll tell you what happens when your body is a new kind, tone young and to be a body that hyperextends, control over your pliable lines and borders, your new lakes and streams? For a while, like how the heat breaks, the air comes through an alley, new fragments shrugged off a relocation, the how-new paradox, a crowd pleaser, predictable novelty. I've danced to that song-and-[   ]. Pliable un-body, piled up, packaged for transport like nothing's happened, nothing ever will. The long-lost narrator returns for a few paragraphs, instills pretend continuity, a mess. Inevitable, and we trust. [Thank you for your]

THE MAKEUP COUNTER

I tell you what:
I live inside a problem.
There are men. Some
of whom. I'm not
excusing myself, but I
am eating several
servings of contiguous
cake. I move from one
city back to my original
idea, which was full
of the evil imaginary
separated, but then.
You see where this is
going. The Florist
comes by
for pearly cheeks, and
I demonstrate
a foolproof method.
The path all, always
the same, equally real
and almost
real. My sales
space is open.

THE BLOGGER

[SUBMITTED PAST MIDNIGHT]

1) Since you asked, I can tell how far into my life I'm getting by the number of vegan multivitamins left in each 90-day bottle— which somehow makes me feel deader, fruitless, though nutritionally buffered.

2) Seventeen, a pinnacle in entertainment retrospect, attention cast eternally toward. What're your cares, depoliticized, and how can we sell them back to you who gives them life.

3) What I've seen is love and loneliness at the same time. Our obsessive municipal production of dotingly salted caramels, luxurious and intellectually uncurious.

4) I'll be named gross for sinking to it, pre-deconstructed wanting, sick-making, a hunger-love, self-starved, mean and immature and incapable, a wet pile of growing and rotting simultaneously. Fantastic. Let's gussy that up, just enough technically proficient graffiti in the banner. Sell it back.

5) I'll get to it, the topic of the day. Have you talked to the Centaur? The Makeup Counter gifts me samples, calls to action, clicks, reassurance like two fingers

drawn   across   the   wrist.

6) When the dreams roll in, donate proceeds.
Keep up the live streamed newsreel, or keep
moving through it like the cartoon jellyfish
you   are,   issuing   orders   dressed
in   soft   silks   and   barren   badges.

Call our bluff collective. But really, what do you want? Who do you like best? Which of these nine adoptable kittens best represents your personality? Tell the Pollster. Who's talking to whose structural social paralysis through a conversational playlist: to socialize, to structure, to paralyze, to playlist. Self-care sales, ourselves on GoPro steady ripping through intersections for the thrill and efficiency of it. Some get stopped more than others. As we grow, Detective—you into me into us—we're all barometers of our hometown attitudes, the comments sections specifically. Who's what to whose righteous safety as we get older and stop making—sorry, lost and sensing stillness—unforgivable acts somehow ignorable in the sick churning of day-to-day quiet [the city is].

But how lost can a true user be while still she holds her searching device skyward for a signal? [The signal is not a story.] The Rider gasps by, encased and glowing. We signal reflexively to the Actuary through our airwaves. When private safety's not public or neither, less sensing. We can't explain this alone and unwatched. Watch us, Detective.

The dressing room full of outfits my colleagues and I put ourselves into: recreationally, protectively, seductively, communicatively. Pinball machines and claw games, the prizes for which make the watching bearable. All the lights, the mechanical whirring thought, we can't do better. Which do you prefer?   I'll   do   it.   We'll   do   it.   Fractured   objects make okay correlatives when you don't care much for their well-being.

The events of the city and surrounding areas as they are reported are good, and they are bad, and they are new and old, and we will discuss everything over rosé spritzers, the way it should be done, road closures, under the table, winking, new recipes for desserts we'll never assemble to sing about off-screen. You understand. The Mayor, though: national aspirations all over her expensive heels. We'll cover her ascension with rounds of thick white, whiter, whitest eyeliner, fingers interlinked behind our collective backs.

THE HOUSEKEEPER

What's to think about. Today, limit interactions.

While cleaning, compose a melody without a song and erase it back to tape hiss or quieter. Place the book, spine up, on the Formica. Write an unnamable mood across one's fists and close. Keep a key, dissipate, a juniper berry on the bare floor in the corner, polished concrete. This space of diffuse light, no shadows, a moderated habitat. Dissociated full-spectrum bulbs in the micro-studio, discreetly fending off disorder as successfully as can be expected. Simple temperature. Indoors. Not too close to the sun.

There's a mountain behind or among or throughout the fog past this window, elevated. I haven't been writing.

My journal hypercultural horticulture, fabrications all literal or less: a thin thread from pothos to philodendron. Dust everywhere like velvet and easy. Not too close to the sun. About to think about what.

But what you said [the city is].

A disorderly happiness may creep through, up the rising vines, dispersing into the light.

Retaken or redrawn, is it dawn drawing
color across the darkened glass buildings
across the street? Is someone in there? [Is it
you,] flash of inspiration? I find myself
trapped here comfortably in my party-
friendly jumpsuit, though mostly I'm asleep
on the couch facing the windows,
which look out on more windows,
stories up, cleanly level.

A starling floats invasively through my view.

Another, aswarm.

There's little other furniture, and I can't
shake these phrases, thoughts, partial,
circling and diving like for a kill. The lens on
the city swings as I see it, and I remember
to carry myself like a man of the future or
in it, then swings again and I forget,
remember when the silence resettles.

I saw them on the news in the bar, waiting
for my pickup after class. I can't make this
clearer: I hadn't paid for a drink
all afternoon. Society stepped up, pulled
its weight for once. I saw that familiar
shadowy silence, slick like satin, drape
down, draw back. I saw [did I, was it you]
the Twins cross the park, hotly anticipated,

a doubled blur on-screen in neon green,
the   press   a   gaggle   trailing—
Journalist   lingering,   fretting   Gardener.

I'm so tired, I raise my left arm above
my   head   in   a   gesture   of   fainting.
Are   you   [still]   watching,   Detective?

The city won't come here, parts of itself cast
off. I'm so tired I let a strip of sunlight fall
across   my   closed   eyes,   reflected
from the facing structure, and it keeps me
awake, clean. And I know I can't, never
could,   correct   any   of   this.

THE FORENSICS TEAM

[In this scene]

The Forensics Team coalesces to place a bromeliad, blue-green variegated, in your cubicle's corner of self-actualization, pitching forth newer shoots [oops] efforts.

Middle-bound as careless lesser sensor green, young grass, wrong colors.

THE PROVOST

Academic institutional late-stage capitalism: the hows and whys of a yellowing apple, revealingly lightweight once unearthed. Coffee? [No thanks,] do other animals bite their tongues, do you think? With such staunch predictability? I prefer vaster, more stately recuperation with spa water and heavy sunk fruit in reception. Strawberry-mango. Oaken paneling. Less outdoors like this, so humid. But really, the ghost I've enlisted to follow me carrying my gown's train gets a paid vacation at the end of the performance. I feel good about their release, my little associate, funding secured, and I move on. What was the question?

THE DREAMBOAT

[SUBMITTED CRYPTOGRAPHICALLY]

: I understand there's no passing
serenely into an ocean from the city, no such
exit like the Weather,
the creeping, peeling silence :

: A finger poised above the delete key, I am
one citizen, tracking, collating,
and deadly dreaming my place among
commerce, I drift, in service of
[this interview is] :

: A citizen only by others' willing
interactions with, I am institutional or
otherwise a brand account,
the inscrutable, a forum for public
participation, full sponcon :

: A particular difficulty, a dreamboat,
when all difficulties blur large into recurrent
reinforced prophesy, embodied as a low
encroaching fog, sequined like
a kid summarizing tactical approaches to
overwhelming geraniums on the sill
grown large and rangy, sticky
fragrance, a stuck-up cover-up :

: My dreamboat memory posits common
knowledge as a fetching vision board,
that after death, the missing ones

collapse into all earlier iterations of
themselves at once, nothing neatly
folded, the prime and decline
mussed and available, sick comfort :

: These collapsed presences lend
themselves to erratic emotional response,
more dreamboats who're me
but slower, less careful in addressing
the public's growing concerns :

: All versions, dreamboats, paused in our
places of work, watchful, fingers
poised over the delete options,
editing sunshowers silver
in the ads we make for ourselves, the only
appropriate metaphor for death
: a chromed ocean, public comment :

THE TELLER

What was the question? I say, To
approach a stranger you've lied
to   outrageously,   age
inappropriately, recently, about
what you're doing in this place:
be   aloof   but   confident.
Have a vape with you. Humor
and heart, says me, the movies,
the   Radio   Producer,
all the paper pop-up guides.
There's a way to become
emotionally   unstunted,   isn't
there?   Mustn't   there   be?
Hand   out   the   bank's   money.
Start   again.
Maybe   do   a   stint   singing
the   company   line,   single
out your dead center, your
disappeared selves, string their
shadows up alternating with
lights slowly, shorting down
the line, but point them toward
those shadowy others who send
you   to   the   vault   for   gold
among   the   angler   fish
in   the   blue   inside.
The Register asks for your social
media   handle,   a   moment,
a memo, the Weather. Well.
Cracked iced tea bottles, empty
prescription tubes, wrappers
and foliage, my tidal feelings,

money running low. They don't belong [here]. I don't. Dreams in insular granite, the sugary credit ones, the runaway ones, then go back to sleep underwater. I can just see you now, Detective. You are calmly, trustingly lit, flashing activated by water, and just like all the people in this bank, bobbing and blinking steadily, buoyed by their hopes of eventual rescue.

THE SHOPPER

Zooming around clad in the voice I've ended up with, ecstatic til the gas runs out, then virtual orange, a warning, dotting the shifting parking lot. You've asked me to describe a visit to the grocery store, an afternoon at work, a weathered wren pecking at a deflated pumpkin as I search for coupons on my phone and yet, here I give in, humming some, but like in the shower, through the audio filter my anatomy makes, a general rugged winking toward remember-the-list. Like a sailor, never. I heard about the Twins summoned to the city; I remember them born. Rings of daisies cropping up in the county. The Impalement Artist stuttering, starlings swarming the Tour Guide.

Adventuresome, a papaya right there among the lemons and poorly lit in this gussied up warehouse packed with other people's toddlers. Stone fruit like body parts, pit centered. A smell like bubblegum and antibacterial foam. Voice, a party trick but pleasant for whom. On Halloween, my thrift falters and so do I, my checkout, my cart a virtual pumpkin orange. A virtual ghost in real-life color, making the best out of a messy situation. Necessary, necessity, edible trinkets. I can only align my expression with yours for so long until I get hungry, tired—same difference—who cares. Sign me up for your loyalty. There's a fading everywhere the city won't stop. Circling the parking lot, front right wheel catching every pebble. I can't live like this, or I can, and I have been. I have been all along.

THE TEMP

[SUBMITTED AS A TIMESHEET]

Work, I know. This knowing: work. This too, knowing work, and so, a nap. Working, my expertise, sort of. A living. The left living? Or, groceries? Most of a week's groceries. Part of most of a week's groceries, oh and a resume entry, reentry, entry, reentry.

A place I go, know, and drink light coffee. A cube of one's own. A germy, fluorescent place. One's bag lunch, Tupperware with mismatched lid, labeled, as if to say, *I* *chose* *this,* *I* *promise.*

A zebra plant, having known no other means of light, flourishes in the northern corner of the assigned desk. A human, having known some other ways of living, eats the loose M&Ms provided in reception. Everywhere, this repeated scene, all cities, recent eras, ultralit like a drug.

What, I know, record. Reinterpretation to excise meaning, black out, forget it, erase parts and make something new, potent, consumable. My living, it's the end of the round wide world. Was this the Actuary's hand I held in yesterday's position or yours, Detective? [The city where] all your questions have been posed and answered, worked over and repurposed. A place I go, I promise, and look no further.

Help, I said help, I said. Help, retreating. To the historical replica mercantile vessel. My body does things that I hate, like, accept. Other. Objects. The sails of which are unexposed, masts axed, plugged into the dock with a long, dirty, yellow cord. I play all the parts. Who are you?

That day the starlings swarmed me. But why do you arrive making such sad sounds?

What else is that the Palm Reader listens to me through the slap of the harbor on the hull. What else is repainted forest. Green. When I seamed the sails I was appreciated. Unaccepted. Gratuities. For me, this is a cage. This, a rope and a bed built into the wall in the cabin.

This is where the fish go. And the sugar. This watery town inviting, us we seal our shutters against the heat. Teenagers crawl past with their demon pets, a camera crew [the   time   when]   [REDACTED]

[The city where]

My boat follows me home on a string, floating, sluggish, asleep through the alleys. You taught me, Detective, to know everyone I? Talk to. But the years ticker tape, and I don't. I tie my replica, loosely, to you—

THE NEOTRANSCENDENTALIST

A mirror outside, set outward
against a stoop, toward
the open instead of opening
a wall like a window, a portal
backward or, with luck, farther
forward repeating. More slow-
growth forest in the alleys,
sidewalk disrupted by unruly
roots, unpeopled, or more
likely the neighborhood still,
maybe more emptied out.
The fences redundant. Some
elk higher up, doubled, set
cleverly backlit before
a wanted presence erased,
easy, deflected or
distracted. The city
center always night,
mirrored and bells.

] [

I wait in my doorway
to transform into a person
whose nothing seeds romance,
whose reluctance turns
reflective and necessary
in spitting rain.

The Cartographer's schematics,
a   gift   left   unwrapped
in the vestibule. A cold new
Victorian whose superstitious
patience   ushers   in
the   outdoors   as   a   prop.
A   bloomer   whose   late
summer turns a sweet result.
Golden   and   monolithic.

THE FORENSICS TEAM

[In this reassessment]

A lousy neon tether spreads laterally, but you draw two fingers, mark
the air, the place you believe to be your corner
of helpful friends and benefactors, holographic.

Chill innards, the flowering still comes [oops] wrong.
There's luxury in all this inner heavy lifting. You wait it out.

THE DESIGNER

World-renowned contemporary Victorian aesthetic,
Romantic even, peach-cinnamon, a shiny hearse.
Millennial pink and Gen Z yellow. Coal accents,
a sunrise more magical, floaty chiffon
in the vampire melee. Help-me vowels, my vendetta
seasonally lacking. A year of the worlds in which
I do not traffic, verb-wise and -ose.
And so many? Disappearing,

I need homebody split-leaf approval, jewel-toned,
my milky head bobbing, effort reporting.
Simple syrup outfitted, crystalline and heels.
My metallic all ironic, I waste here on this fainting couch,
inducing hypnosis as a substitute for interaction.
Type courageous, a flagrant rattan headband bow.
The teenagers surrounding my apartment in tune with
their emotional impulses, distractingly fashionable,
harmonic—not a symphony, something bigger, silent,
adorning city buses like diamonds.

An accordion wends away down the street
toward the park with the cardinal fountains,
west a dancer en pointe on the shell of a tortoise,
misting salted honey water, super bougie. [The dream
where] [the hour when] [the city in which] [you didn't
expect me here, did you, as] this year's canary, despite
or beside the quartz, explicitly died. Jungle without
the humidity, sweater weather. If you, you, my
alter ego, my muse, my cipher, your work, my
satisfactory digestion and excretion of. Daily
dressing the Ingenue, who expertly preens.

Lacking, go to sleep. The shop window will open again at 9:30 a.m. tomorrow, as if that meant anything to one so determined to dream sweaty, buried in humus: you, Detective. You wear it so well.

THE NOSTALGIST

Define   anhedonia: personal
collage,   a   perfect   summer   day.

Self-expression   radically   regressing.   Irreversible.   Okay.
It   used   to   be   all   sorts   of   personal   sadnesses   were
colorful: wine   reds,   bruise   purples,   blood
blushes,   oversaturated,   crushed
velvet—my   Internist,   she   slept.

Already   a   city   disease   as   imminent   as,   only
as   regressive   as,   one's   own   system   to   fight
against   or   give   in   to   inner   romance.
The   monument   glows   on   weeknights
now,   signals   indecipherable   [the   story   is].

Built   the   limbo   into   black   light: rural.   Pushing   aggressively
ahead   into   code-sleep,   subdivision   of   tensely   concatenated
body   borders,   then   relief.

Speech   to   become   one   plane,   clear,   then   re-splits,   the   fracture
will   be   as   endless,   from   code   to   language
to   tune   to   language   to
code   to   pictography.   Symbols   resound
around   the   city   center.

We   are   learning   to   be   cleaner,   nondisruptive,   seamless,
bottomlessly   hopeful   giving   in,   split   lips   through

walls of ocean. We called for the Twins to wander the city,
imagined our future in nighttime metropolis complexions.
We got ahead of ourselves.

We were learning to stay awake because we had drugs enough
for it. Me? I never had that kind of community.

Living part-time personas, a virtual I here, ignorant.
Define clutter: say it the same,
and then say it again.

THE COPS

[out of pocket since]   [on administrative leave for]

THE IMPALEMENT ARTIST

Not here for the show? [Starts in five.]

When my magic makes such measly, what, said shoddy miracles: a single blade of grass longer than the rest of the patch in the park, piss-ready, a blade single steel and longer and pinned in the bull's-eye in drywall above my head, vibrating still—

Ta-da, like my teeth says, TA-DA, I said, I said my taut magic falters before the knife my neck's meant for, fingertips, oh, resigned, is reassigned, or is my death today not worth the spectacle or worthy—

When I painted the circles in circles in circles, my Tour Guide, my Dancer, they asked. [Are you watching?] I dragged an index slowly across each wrist, and they left me alone. Or were encumbered by the prospect of becoming an audience, or were pulled into the streetlight's humid cone illuminated by rain—

Was that light life magnetic, majestic? Was it illusory? What's the difference? I've found belief like a shiny quarter in the fountain—

The city in love with its waterfront, reserves it for tourists sent down by the Concierge, lining up for rides on the comedy speedboat. And no one stops them, even when the fog—

Even when the kid juggling fire in the amphitheater on a shitty unicycle, his condo's for short sale, is in flames—

But you already know what the audience comes for—don't

you—not the magic.

THE TRANSPLANT

Here's a thing no one knows: rainy today, my birthday again, and I've forgotten [the memory is not a dream where] I search a scorched city, exploded glass lanterns scattered, cracked revolving doors and shifting stone passageways. Here, a staircase descending from thunder, a mission I knew the name of once and forgot as I went, climbing chain-link, pressing palms to netted trees, building fires, opening portals by answering riddles wrong and salty, just like old times, the fog comes coursing through.

If you give an up, a glass pavilion in the park, emptied of its protected species, given up a nod inside one, a simple silver balloon released up into a cache of memories to drift against the glass until the cold, inevitable, shrinks it, returns to you that way, disappeared reflection.

All my friends light galleries, festivals, words never phrases. And so never to pinpoint this pervasive disorientation, a lark: my joke and joke again, a love, lofted, fell again, rose and died again in a garden full of them, *plein de* bushy royalty so humdrum in their eventual execution. Galleries and gardens. I don't live here except when I do, in a shadow cast by those the Dreamboat's always describing as neighbors to us who know better: the darkening, the disappearances, the fog.

You, Detective, your investigation, a splinter in a primary limb ignored, and now it's part of you [don't you], and you love it like a part of you, like you could kill it if you were finally courageous.

To keep raking one's arms across the roses, florets bloom out like data points on a graph: trending. This city, its fountains, its nights, small data. Its murals of heroes and flowers. Its passing silences in between car stereos, club music, its sodium lights, its following me home, its parks, concrete cracked, its empties, its trash eaten by a beautiful, caring monster, a system, cobbled from the vials up, here and here and here you love and can't claim and wouldn't but.

I can't face it, or can, canting, drawing my own face in blue eyeliner in as many seconds as it takes to dismantle my inherited hold on what everyone else needs. Erase the hold without a memento to remember. Better. Okay.

THE POLLSTER

[SUBMITTED UNSOLICITED]

Dear Detective, please consider carefully:

- ☐ What if no one's ever called you openhearted
- ☐ How will you go on
- ☐ Which chakra for better cleansing
- ☐ What if no one's ever called you an old soul
- ☐ Should your feelings be hurt
- ☐ Mine or [the answers are]
- ☐ Flyers across the city's listing telephone poles

To clarify: answer as though I were you or vice versa; whichever. These surreal absolutes are so 2007. Truth or don't care? You understand:

- ☐ What if I'm not sure I have feelings
- ☐ Will I be able to opt out if I decide later I don't deserve the upgrade
- ☐ What if your cat is your best friend, but your other cat is the one with the pervasive social media presence
- ☐ What if the boundary between the city and the desert surroundings were wider, less like dipping into and out of a municipal pool
- ☐ How much live streaming is too much live streaming
- ☐ What if you only make art your friends like
- ☐ My friends [the answers are]
- ☐ What if you only friend art you like making
- ☐ Whose resolute apocrypha

Answer as though you were you but eighteen months from now. You understand:

- [ ] What if it were your kid every time, every time the city goes silent
- [ ] What if all your utopian ideals are subconscious or only expressed through a desire against what's missing in your current circumstances
- [ ] How long is elliptical, and how do you get into getting into it
- [ ] What if too glib is not glib enough, or vice versa; whichever, who cares
- [ ] How do I know none of my neighbors, geographic or otherwise
- [ ] How many times a day do you look in the mirror and wish for a future in which the collective subsumes all but the smallest parts of the individual

Answer as though you want me to understand you or myself; whichever:

- [ ] How do you look in this hat
- [ ] What about a shaved head
- [ ] On a leash
- [ ] Where do I go after work to forget I've been at work
- [ ] What if you left the city whenever you wanted
- [ ] Wanted what
- [ ] What if at the tops of the mountains there's always snow and a portal to some other dimension with better health care
- [ ] Would you support [the questions are]
- [ ] If I'm able to get to the portal without too much fuss, should I go through with it

Just kidding.

☐ What if too glib is

Answer as though I'm not being paid for this and neither are you.

THE FORENSICS TEAM

[In this version]

The Forensics Team, later on, tells the current, collapsed, gone-dead you to care, a repeating pattern [red-blue-rose] scaling brick, because they care where you came from, look into, mark. They're sorry for your [ ]

THE INDUSTRIAL ARCHITECT

If only an _[X]_ distracted by arrangement, if only
my eyelashes singed clean by work, arrangement,
this like no one remembers training regression.
It's hard to see my own complicity, so I don't
usually.   I   just   walk   around.

] [

Heated enough, rearranging love and money, which
is never one thing, and there is always too much of it
somewhere else, and even so. Cheap. I am learning
what it is to have friends and to stay in when it's hot
and to go to a dark bar when it's hot and to stay in
the cities I've chosen to live. When I said money, I
meant   work,   the   products   of   which—got   it.
Some love. Languages condensed back to symbol
and   then   expanded   to   give   proper   warning
as   interactive.   An   accurate   prediction   of   rain.

] [

A symbol for a flower, which is a symbol for an entry.
I've been hired to design a landscape of enormous
thorns to encircle the city, jagged and menacing, so

the danger rumbles impenetrably even if its niceties are not understood. Ten thousand future years of landscape designed to turn away on purpose, regression. I do my small part.

Like a monolith pretending at pheromones, burying the lede, markers infinite
blood-thinner reveries.   I   forge   discovery,   my   designs   for   you,
[the   disappearances   are]   your   quest.

I can spell, make spells, modest itch and sleeping, which fetching display,
witchy   one,   stay   out.

I know who did it, some, covert keep telling into the fog-spread transverse
cruiser   headlamps,   chopper   spotlights,   upheaved   asphalt,   vent   of
acrid   steam   from   the   winter   sewer.

As   interest   wanes,   some   months   distracted,   my   resurfaced   reluctance
revolving   like   lights   on
a   plow   shouldered   over   in   a   storm.   I   did   it,
I   didn't   and   wish   I   did,   I   did.

Blue and rose and clear and red and blue again,
the spins said. Move along, bystander, keep your stories to yourself.
[The answer is] sleeping half in daylight, my half-light omniscience,
floodlights like the Weather across the neighborhood.

Highway, no sleep, quiet smoothed over by traffic, a particular kind
of silence, the copter keeps circling. The Third Shift lets out. I remember
and gather my spells for the next.

THE THIRD SHIFT

On   the   way
home, here where
the   rushing's
traffic,   sewer,
regrettable.
Switch   from
sodium   to
compact
fluorescent   but
purpler, kills the
slick heat like a
kiss to a fistfight
in an alley a few
blocks   off   the
boardwalk.   Fire
escapes   and
dumpsters.   Like
a flat, silver moth,
gold   all   on
the   wet   street
and   sometimes
that   tender
back   of   hand.

Wet   alkaline
keeps crittering,
carries   city
silence,   which—
enough
already—isn't
silence   and   so

imparts no
insight. Some
familiar party
song, it's the way
it is everywhere
[the end is].
Quiets louder
when forcing
into open fact
one's
metaphorical
heart, which—
enough
already—not
even close or
exactly that
desultory,
embarrassing,
deinstitutional-
ized, isolated in
sandy soil. This is
not where I am
but where I live
sometimes. This
isn't my stop
yet, but I'm
getting there.

THE CARTOGRAPHER

Dear [   ], Might it be
so   that   I   always
remember the watery
emergence of waking
to   the   world   this
morning, even from
light nightmares, my
sticky   horoscope:
[an   unreal   dream
where] [an unreal city
where]   everything's
unreal   and
crisscrossed   by
yellow,   rusting
gondolas   swinging
between   roofs,
colliding with sky-
high   construction
cranes   every
direction   across
town,   gentle
undulations   as
the cables sag and rise.
Below   jammed
streets,   underground
passageways
connect institutional
museums   blooming
open opposing ends
of the city, lovingly
curated   installations

of light and chrome
and copper, everyone
losing   their   way.

For the memory of the experience of exertion, I leave my city temporarily to scale a snowy mountain in July. Tall spiders darting around exposed boulders, lichen green, ruddy orange. I rest. I return to find nothing changed in my apartment, cat blinking awake.

Eat a full meal. Days bleed out into nothing. Modified methods for getting leaner, controlling one's menstrual cycles, decontaminating water. Zinc and magnesium to support cleaner dreaming. Less TV. More TV. Less thinking about it.

I spot a burly white mountain goat drinking snowmelt, a herd of elk climbing a steep incline toward tree cover, shrubs with light new leaves, winter-hardened branches, endless episodes of ageless prestige streaming

but for the reassuring imposed discipline of the satellites, where they'll reach and where they won't. Luxuries hulking over my shoulders until I've consumed them. Exotic fruit and chocolate bars. The relief of the loss when you're sure where you are.

[Animal smell from nearby, black shards in the mountain willow]

Sleeping unbundled like a drunk. A new DM from the Adjunct about subletting. Ruly memories. No new articulable understandings. Single observation and on to the next.

To live in a place so full of space, I wander unnoticed. I forget the disappearances until I don't.

To the left and right and ahead, ghost towns in structural collapse, reintegration to a different, older system. Abandoned highway tunnel, graffiti'd in blues and blacks. Me, halfway through.

THE FORENSICS TEAM

[In this dream]

You draw many Xs down the front of your throat with your bruised
index   [red-blue-rose],   and   the   ambulances
just   keep   going   by.

Red spread across leaves in sharp, passing streaks. You leave
a   message   for   us   behind   a   mercury   mirror.

Lateral   siren,   unrooted,   the   other   option,   natural   pale
tillandsia terrarium: anemic tips point, and you draw a line,
decidedly,   from   inner   wrist   to   crook   of   arm.

Red middle [oops] bloom like the inner [oops] petals where
every ghost you know reboots, bored or finally found out.

THE GROUNDSKEEPER

Being away from love, or away being from love, a way of recasting purpose, productivity in artsy free afternoon light, confuses signs from the natural world: the direction of the week's wind, a brush fire down valley that ashes a dead stripe into the hill, emotional themes in movies and music as suggested by corporate algorithms, those most natural and available of petty horoscopes. A predictably botanical ars poetica in overgrown lavender and borage—I maintain.

One sits, watches investigatory teenagers and their entourage trample a path over ditch diversions, the Runner circling cynical sprinklers, is confronted through song with the concept of an unbreakable heart, ungetdownable. Its edges pleasingly rounded, like a worry stone, but what's more romantic: something fragile, marred, or the same thing made permanent? There're two ways to stay undead: invincibility or implacable malleability, and I choose, my city chooses, the one I left. Gothic sun only bearable for so long. I start sweating down the insides of my thighs and turn my head north, wishing some beauty or a thin sheet of rain might swish around in my wake like a sour smell. I've left, chosen, but keep an ear back toward my ticker-tape heart.

THE OPENING ACT

I keep hoping for a wolf,
stationary or stalking a fawn.
Remnant snow and twig and
high prairie grass pressed in
the direction of wind, even still
when nothing moves. I know
where I am outside the city,
ghost towns intended to lure
the missing. It's hard to
imagine all this gold stranding
as green in warmer months.
Isn't it always like that,
the   potential,   matted
and majestically spotlit as
the   afternoon   wears   on
til   its   closure.   What
was   the   question?

THE VISITOR IN THE HILLS

Last chance to take a walk or type. And how. A familiar view either way, one less replicable. Carrot cake for communal breakfast, everyone distractible. Not considering who's talking to whom, I feel hot. I'll go back to my trap. A pretty staging area's a greenroom anywhere, never calm. My boss's boss's HR representative suggests we all speak obliquely, but all day it's already troublesome. Weirdly elusive. Finding a new home takes longer when you know you'll be retreating: a dictum.

There's a photo of me in the visitor scrapbook, which gestures toward perpetuity while enacting purposeful forgetfulness. Or, it makes me feel nervous all over, watching shadows under the front door. Or, forgetfulness gins up generosity, either through intention or forgiveness. So, better, maybe erasure's a closer? An image to be skimmed past. A person [a sign, a symbol, a city, a dream] at a desk, smiling, document on-screen on-screen. Scenery unless it ever becomes evidence, unlikely.

Windows on three sides, a wide, stable sightline, except once I start feeling queasy there's no coming back from it but through sleep, which comes with difficulty. My face is the absolute worst version of itself and stays that way despite all the attention I have paid, paid for, am paying. It blurs the speaking, the world, the woulds. The hay in the field is beautiful, and the stretch of painted bench along the edge of the patio makes shadows that are angular but soft. I will take a picture, and later I will forget these nerves, this relief. To be leaving. To have left.

THE CRONE

We   were
alone   [   ]
We
decided   to
[   ]   Be
more   alone
[   ]
Senseless
and yet [   ]
There   we
were
pilfering   [
]   Witchy
wailing [   ]
Wildly
postured
and
watching
this   [   ]
Newly
expanding
onyx   aura   [
]   Come
down   from

] [

Wild   green
resuming
preps   an
exit [   ] A
remainder
for   [   ]
Synapse
twitch
downed
lines   [   ]
You   ask   [
]   Instead
of   memory
I   found
there   [   ]
A   round
clear   gap   [
]   A   stream
spilling
broadly
over [   ] A
pebbly   lot
overgrown
[   ] Two
girls   me
reversed,
doubled   [
]   I
explained   [
]

] [

The   park
below [   ]
The   city
opens   like
a pool [   ]
Brimming
with
what's   left
it   [   ]
Observant
around
the [   ]
Edges   a
round [   ]
Clear gap [
] Or mirror
if   missing
becomes   [
]   Content
as   last
night's
silences   [
]   How
disappear
-ance   and
forgotten   [
]

] [

Unsure   [   ]
Every
night   [   ]
Shadow
skitter   [   ]
Below   I
miss   my
answers   at
arms   [   ]
Length   a
relief   [   ] A
round   clear
[   ] Gap   a
smoothed
slick
remember
-ing   [   ]
The   city
before
me
dissolves
into
daylight   [
]

THE MISANTHROPE

You, you have angry blood. You have
angry blood and a smile, of course, sunny
moments of none of these peppy people
who moved here from elsewhere to satisfy
their art experience. Clouds finally come in
after days of vampire sun, relentless,
burning off the fog, application downloads
and politics, towering atmospheric relief
hung up at a distance, rain the next valley
over but not here. Self says, It's okay that I
don't want to listen to your description of
the body's lower functions, and today
I mean it.

When the dead rose, rise again in a garden
full of them, but how do you master
the responsible party, at the party
ungetdrunkable and the impossible weight
of careful behavior like that for a decade.
Decide, [do you] a flower, but ultimately
I'm in it now, part of the sun all hours
and invincible.

[ ]
Too far from the original concept and not
close enough to the next, anew, a view so
big the sunset wraps around the whole sky
like a film, a haze, a new kind of fog,
deadening submission. Every day
a reminder of the cardinal directions,
that close mountain, that hill, the earth
a crossable plane away outside my gridded

city I still see the peaks of through, surrounding sun and sun and sun til there's not. I miss the evenings.

[ ]

When I left I thought an outside perch, a shook-up surrounding might gift a new perspective, but I'm ever missing the perspective from inside, which I never really had, real like real, my nonnative privileges. This, my trip:

The Resident. The Vacationer. The Self-Segregator. The Removed. The Willingly, Willfully Exiled.

Record the day-to-day in ugly text and collect some easy, evasive dialogue. Self shops for workout clothes, leggings and breathable tops, at the outlying mall on the weekend. The only utopia is this, and it's everyone's fault. Self's card is not often declined. Self sometimes speeds through the early seconds of reds and hasn't been pulled over in years. Self's credit, for now, is stable. Self is pre-approved for a mortgage. Self's body, while in predictably disappointing decline, still, for now, has not disappeared, for whatever that's worth. Read: some. Eats sandwiches and uses the air conditioner as modestly as the heat allows. Needs and is provided with more alone

time, flexible core hours at work. Distance
like benzodiazepine.

[ ]
It's always been true that the best kind of
circus is the opposite of a circus: small
nothing movements coordinated quietly by
a central processor. In truth, a symphony.
The same is not true for cities, the best
kinds. If only it were me.

THE RINGMASTER

[OVERHEARD]

Blue bleeds process all over the picnic, party
beasts circling. Blood smells adventurous,
blue, new, ambitious. I've missed all of you so
much even though or because you kept
circling without me, camouflaged in timber
but for the eyes. Your vigilance is its own red
reward up here in the sunset mountains.

I've done my time in the dunk tank
and emerged unscathed but coated: sweat and
dew. Squirrels chattering from aspens, robins
prancing, cardinals red ambulance sirens
everywhere in the dawn parking lot. Everyone
I know shows up everywhere, but I know
the commitment's a lie, which I take
as a compliment I remember receiving after
the content evaporates before me like steam.
Slippery blue, soul-stealing applause that it is.

My constitution flickers and goes dark,
standing on a wire, connection like liquid
conduction and harsher. I'm trying really
hard to be respectable nowadays, more blue.
Sending my animals out over the hills, sending
my girls to the city to help. It feels like
I'm trying really hard to be respectable.
Standing on half my available legs, a star,

a feeling, sustained engagement, and I've not
yet   caught   up   to   altruism.

You   beasts   huff   and   snort   and   join
back in the routine, though none of us knows
exactly why we have to destroy the city
that feeds us. I sometimes let other ghosts
through doors ahead of me just to be purplish,
nice.   I'd   never   want   to
make   anyone   late.   If   you   see
them down there with their demons, tell them
we   haven't   forgotten.   Tell   them
we're   on   our   way.

THE GARDENER

This, welcome to: a dirty blank.
Drawn and charted, a tight circle of
Gravel. Botanical theme
Regression, several dis-
Appointments and their relief
Track quick plot abandonment, mark its
Divergences and eventual returns in
Gullies. [In this space,] a small fountain of
Concrete. Permanent seasonal
Arrangement disorder. The Dancer
En pointe.

Here, I've buried a single peony
Bloom, knowing nothing will
Change I won't draw growing down
Or into. I pace the lot through the heat
Always pouring, filling divots, slicking air
Greenish, juicing trash in the sun steamy.
I take cover as the Twins drift adeptly by.
Uncomfortable investigations in nature,
My role: a gutter, detached.

Fat flies and drums of municipal water.
Is this a city or a house, a home
Or a camp? Laws or rules, roles or
Honor? Myself or who. Less
The heat's damage, inevitably.
All my options.

THE FORENSICS TEAM

[In this reckoning]

Eventually, the light comes to you. Will they speak?

You will likely keep breathing if you go outside.

You can't get close to the ghosts anymore.

They've moved on.

THE DETECTIVE

You're dreaming
You're asking questions

You're asking one question over and over
You're not sure you're dreaming

You're a killer but not an assassin
You're dyeing your hair blond, and you're concerned about the
        timing

You're destroying a city, a partnership
You're sinking through cool blue jelly

You're alluring and humiliating
You're touching others' lips with your dun thumb

You're embarrassing the suspects who know you best
You're staring at something until you forget it's not yours

You're staring at something until you forget it's not part of you
Forgetting your complicity is one problem

You're awake in the city
The city is not a story

You're from somewhere you're returning to
Trying to climb a hill and can't, sunk to all four hooves

A tower of apartments lists westward and blinks
Forgetting the difference between acknowledging and winking

You're responsible
Your city is transparent, shadeless, and cluttered

Performing one task at a time protected by tropical plants in terra-
          cotta pots
You're identifying protective corners in your workspace

Falling asleep without sound surrounding
Not waking yourself howling, your partner

Falling asleep without the television on
You're forgetting to eat

You're building a dream from a metaphor
You're always forgetting to always be joking

You're accompanied by ghosts who follow you like crows through the
          city, cobbled, bustling, bright with silver balloons
The city morphs to a desert mesa with sagebrush and bighorns

The sun is turning the earth inhospitable
You are turning the earth inhospitable

You're building a story from dismantled symbols
The ghosts become a greenish fog, watery

The city's central fountain overflows with bubbles and coins at
          midnight
Beckoned, you're eating fatty cakes and fruit pastries and are joyful

The ghosts who follow you become a silent dog
The ghosts become a moth

The ghosts become a woven hat tied round your chin as you pick your
       way through a misty vineyard, neon leaves, lilting toward a
       farmhouse-cum-celebrity restaurant
Altering the constellations to revivify your love

All lights pointing toward your new goals, revivified
The content skipping and buffering and keeps buffering

You are represented everywhere you look and yet
Finding established trails in the wilderness, relief and disappointment,
       an animal smell

You're moving toward a vacant lot
The crowd coming together to form a lake

The day beginning to end and panic bubbling up
It's night and you can't sleep

You're lying to everyone you know
You're listening and misrecording

Prone, giving the benefit of the doubt to the one warm part of the
       villain
Your hair stops falling out

You're no longer disordered
You're falling asleep in rooms of mansions managed for tourists
       to solve mysteries in: condemned mental institutions,
       grand hotels, shuttered cinemas, brick alleys, all climate-
       controlled and carefully surveilled, passageways just wide
       enough to admit a human body successfully

Leaving something, a ring, in one of the rooms of the mystery house
Enacting the mystery through your search and retrieval

Waking up in a new place over and over until the waking's no longer
   new
The earth so dry it turns to dust and hovers, suffocating

You're watching satellites sail through space all night from your roof,
   still recording
Voices telling you to get in the pool, and you do, the rungs of the
   ladder rough gold all the way down

ACKNOWLEDGMENTS

Much gratitude to the editors of the following journals, where some of these poems first found homes, often in different versions: *Oversound*, *Denver Quarterly*, *Pinwheel*, *Iowa Review*, *Vinyl*, *Tupelo Quarterly*, *Conjunctions*, *Baltimore City Paper*, and *Prelude*.

For ghost town investigation company and general radness, thanks to William Brown. For time and encouragement, thanks as always to Micah Bateman and Steven Kleinman. For finding this book a home, thanks to Jeannie Vanasco, literary citizen bar none. For support while writing this book, thanks to the Ucross Foundation and to the Robert W. Deutsch Foundation. For generous attention and care, thanks to Marisa Siegel and everyone at Northwestern University Press.

Never for money, always for love: Nate MF Brown.